MW00582204

Coulter & Payne
Farm Distillery's

101 Uses for Moonshine

CHRIS BURNETTE &
ELISE COULTER BURNETTE

Foreword by Donald Snyder

4880 Lower Valley Road • Atglen, PA 19310

Copyright Notice
Credits and Disclaimers

Other Schiffer Books on Related Subjects:
Distilling Fruit Brandy (Josef Pischl) ISBN: 978-0-7643-3926-4

Copyright © 2016 by Chris Burnette and Elise Coulter Burnette
Library of Congress Control Number: 2016931349

Designed by John P. Cheek
Cover design by Matt Goodman
Type set in Alice/Bembo Std

ISBN: 978-0-7643-5117-4
Printed in China

Published by Schiffer Publishing, Ltd.
4880 Lower Valley Road
Atglen, PA 19310
Phone: (610) 593-1777; Fax: (610) 593-2002
E-mail: Info@schifferbooks.com
Web: www.schifferbooks.com

For our complete selection of fine books on this and related subjects, please visit our website at www.schifferbooks.com. You may also write for a free catalog.

Schiffer Publishing's titles are available at special discounts for bulk purchases for sales promotions or premiums. Special editions, including personalized covers, corporate imprints, and excerpts, can be created in large quantities for special needs. For more information, contact the publisher.

We are always looking for people to write books on new and related subjects. If you have an idea for a book, please contact us at proposals@schifferbooks.com.

Opposite: The distillery staff admiring "Dolly," Coulter & Payne Farm Distillery's 150-gallon, electric, bain marie, hybrid column still. Pictured are Chris Burnette, President and Head Distiller; Cole Uphouse, VP of Production; Amanda Snyder, VP of Administration; and Josh Hackmann.

Dedication

This book is dedicated to the men and women of the *Coulter & Payne Farm Distillery*, its customers, and our family. May we all continue to make the world a better place one drink at a time.

Contents

Moonshine in a mason jar immediately after distillation.

Foreword

"Patience. Sustainability. Tradition. Family. Responsibility. Oh, and corn." These are the ingredients Chris told me when I first asked him what went into his whiskey. Little did I know how true it was.

When Chris and Elise asked me to write the foreword for this book, I didn't know what to say. We have been friends and colleagues for several years and I had learned quite a bit about them, but had no idea what really went into their process or why. As I dove deeper into understanding them and finding out what made them do what they do, I found their corn is just one of many important ingredients in their whiskey. But that, too, is shaped by their philosophy.

As an industry insider for over a decade, I have worked with countless distilleries, suppliers, and vendors. Some of them have been young and growing; many have been around for decades or longer. For many of the larger, established distilleries, the bottom line guides their every decision. Not so for Chris and Elise from Missouri; for them, the bottom line is only part of the conversation.

That is what made my conversation with Chris and Elise so fascinating. They knew so much about the industry, but they were still a bit on the outside. A small, craft producer in a world dominated by huge conglomerates. A producer that not only makes their spirits, but also grows their own ingredients. They are entirely vertically integrated in a world of outsourcing. Three years ago this was unheard of, yet they do not back down.

In fact, they keep pushing the merits of their traditional processes and philosophy while reintroducing traditions that fell off decades, if not centuries, before. In this way they are mavericks. They are the outsiders who are reshaping what it means to produce a farm-to-bottle, artisanally distilled spirit. They are showing the world the value of the family farm, the importance of being stewards of the land, and the value of its people.

In an industry dominated by conglomerates local craft spirits have an uphill climb. Chris and Elise are outliers in an outsource-dominated industry, but are trying to bring back long-forgotten core values. With their help, we will rediscover the traditions that made our country great and that make American-made spirits so wonderful.

Donald Snyder
Founder and Principal,
Whiskey Systems Online and Whiskey Resources, LLC

Acknowledgments

We are extremely thankful for the generous support of our community in Missouri, Northern Georgia, and Eastern Tennessee. The people of Appalachia and the ozarks have been incredibly supportive and eager to help us in our endeavor. Without judgment they have offered us information, help, support, and, most importantly, great food and 'shine.

One of the welcome signs to Shawnee Bend Farms, the authors' 200-acre family farm in Union, Missouri.

We want to thank our family and friends who have supported us from the beginning. We can't list everyone that has helped us, but know that we could not have done this without you. You know who you are. We love you!

The members of Coulter & Payne have been integral to writing this book. They have supported us through the entire process and without their help we would not have finished it! We are a small group, but it includes the employees, board members, shareholders, and extended family. Since we are a family business they are all family and we love them dearly.

We would also like to thank our son, Henry, for putting up with us as we worked to not only write this book, but put together our family business. One day, he will come in to his own as a leader in our community. Until then, he is subject to our failures and successes, our moments of psychosis and clarity, our unreasonable expectations, and our unwillingness to give up. Good luck with that! We love you.

The main driveway and only entrance to Shawnee Bend Farms and the Distillery, Union, Missouri. The farm is surrounded on three sides by the Bourbouse River in Franklin County, Missouri.

Coulter & Payne Farm Distillery's Barrel House and Barn at Shawnee Bend Farms in Union, Missouri.

Introduction

Being raised in the Appalachian Mountains and now living in the ozarks, I have come to understand my roots are always with me. Even more than that, my family's roots are always underfoot. I left home early, trying to get away from the "shackles" of East Tennessee, but I grew up and realized I really didn't want to lose this culture; I just wanted to make my own way. I was bull-headed, stubborn, and independent. Its funny how this stubborn streak—indicative of Scots-Irish ancestry—would force me away, just to have me come railing back.

I unknowingly married a girl from the Ozarks who had the same problem. I fell in love with a stubborn, Scots-Irish (and German) woman who thought very similarly to myself. But the draw to an older time did not stop there. We constantly heard stories from one side of our family that seemed quite familiar to the other. Of course, there are big differences in culture—city versus country, Midwest versus East, and rich versus poor—but at the heart was a familiarity we just could not shake. The more we looked into it, the more we learned Ozark culture is an offshoot of Appalachian. Many of the same stories permeate the hills. Many of the recipes are similar, if not the same. Our families, although very different and with strikingly different experiences, had at their root a shared cultural dimension that drew both of us in.

Elise and I are co-owners—along with several other family members and close friends—of a small farm distillery in Missouri. Our first product was a moonshine made from scratch. We grow the corn; cook, mash, and ferment the beer; distill the alcohol; and even hand-bottle and label the finished product. It is a modern version of a farm distillery from over a hundred years ago. As such, we have a lot of moonshine laying around and get to talk to all kinds of people about its history, uses, tastes, and appeal.

One day, while driving from my hometown in Tennessee back to our current home in Missouri, Elise turned to me and said, "I wonder how many different ways we could use our moonshine?" The idea for this book was born. We wanted to put down not only the current common uses for moonshine, but some of the

Opposite: 1965 Deutz tractor ready to begin plowing a field to plant rye at Shawnee Bend Farms, Union, Missouri.

more obscure and forgotten from our shared culture. We have included the basic, the obscure, the outright strange, and a few cocktail recipes from our distillery.

While most people don't think twice about drinking or using alcohol, many people in our family and those we talk with, including the areas where we grew up, are very sensitive about it. Even if alcohol did not upset them, being highlighted in a book did. Because of this, we have left out any reference to a particular family. Most of the moonshine uses in this book will be attributed to my imaginary "grandmother" to spare anyone embarrassment or unease. Even when I say "my family" I may be talking about someone else or their family. In most cases, the promise of anonymity was required to get the recipe or description. We made a promise to them all and we will take it to our graves!

We hope you like reading this as much as we enjoyed writing it. As we say often: We want to make the world a better place, one drink at a time. Enjoy.

Chris Burnette

Read at your own risk. Do not try these uses at home.
Sarcasm is a genetic trait and possibly a defective mutation.
Please drink responsibly.

Chapter One
A Short History of Moonshine

Whether it's called Moonshine, Likker, Corn Whiskey, Hooch, White Lightning, XXX, 'Shine, 'Snort, Snake Juice, White Dog, Thunderwater, Firewater, Rocket Fuel, or Liquid Courage, the term "Moonshine" has quite a history. Images of car racing, backwoods stills, bathtub gin, mobsters, and mountain people permeate the scene. Tales of illicit activities and outright defiance of the law are considered the norm, as is the defiance of the people who participate.

But what is Moonshine? Some will argue it is illicit or illegal whiskey, regardless of the ingredients used. Others argue it describes a certain type of product, whether legal or not, including corn whiskey, white dog whiskeys, grain-neutral spirits (not a whiskey), and other non-whiskey products. The truth is somewhere in the middle. Traditionally, moonshine—legal or not—is a predominantly corn-based whiskey, including corn whiskeys and white dog whiskeys with a large percentage of corn. Most moonshine distilleries produce a corn whiskey. Under current US law, corn whiskey is one that contains an all-grain mash bill of at least 80% corn and if aged, must be aged in an un-charred barrel. The barrel can be used or new, unlike bourbon, which must be aged in a new, charred oak barrel. White dog whiskeys—traditionally an un-aged bourbon or rye whiskey—are new to the marketplace, as these are normally barrel-aged prior to sale.

Corn whiskey has been a staple of the American experience since the first European settlers came to the New World. Predominantly from Scotland, Germany, and Ireland, many early settlers brought with them the art of distilling. Corn, or maize, was a plentiful crop in the New World and barley was harder to grow. Farmers in the New World—particularly the Scots who settled in the Appalachian Mountains—would distill their grains to carry them to market; a gallon of corn whiskey was much easier to carry than a bushel of corn. It also earned a higher price at the market. In bad crop years, sometimes the only way to offset losses was to turn what was left into whiskey. This was not a way to make extra cash, it was a way to survive. This skill was passed down from father to son, in some cases for nearly 300 years. After the Revolutionary War—fought over paying taxes to the British—the United States government began taxing all alcohol production to pay for the war. Many of the new citizens refused to pay taxes on it and hid their production from the government, and the first moonshiners were born, as was the first revolt against the new American government: The Whiskey Rebellion.

Early in our country's history many farmers would distill local crops into spirits. By the 1830s, there were nearly 20,000 legal distilleries in the United States; most of these were small farm distilleries. They grew their own grain, mashed and distilled it, and took it to market or sold it to locals. By Prohibition this number had dropped to around 1,000 due to mergers, competition, and infrastructure advancements. For the first time, you could get your whiskey from anywhere in the country and small producers could not keep up with larger companies. Some of these went underground along with the already illegal Appalachian Mountain moonshiners to avoid taxes and what they considered a restriction on their rights as Americans. This mentality continues to this day, as does the production of illegal whiskey.

Prohibition was a windfall for moonshiners! Since there were few legal sources of alcohol—mainly medicinally marketed products—moonshine sales skyrocketed. This did not bother many of the mountain moonshiners; they were already skirting the law, but many more began to get in on the action. Some of these producers were heartless, blending methanol and other clear poisons to increase their yield or using automobile radiators without cleaning them out to cool the distillate. These unscrupulous producers produced a product that could possibly kill you, or leave you blind. Many of the mountain moonshiners pushed back by maintaining quality and thus their customer base. They provided hooch to their family and friends and did not want them hurt. Nonetheless, mountain moonshine took a hit and to this day, many people still equate moonshine with a strong and possibly deadly inferior product. It didn't help that Revenuers would spread lies, telling people that any illicit whiskey would kill you; in one case—if it is true—a Revenuer agent added poison to barrels of whiskey to make them undrinkable. As a side note, many of these moonshiners, scrupulous or not, began to modify their cars to outrun the "Revenuers" and get their products to market. This was the birth of Nascar. More than one commercial moonshine producer plays on this to market their product.

What happened to the illegal moonshiner? According to the Division of Alcohol, Tobacco, and Firearms, by the 1980s, the number of illegal stills being seized saw a major decline. This decline matches a more disturbing declining trend in American Folk traditions. After World War II a significant change in the rural culture took place. In large part due to the influence of the GI Bill, many of the young men who served in the war moved out of Appalachia and rural areas into more urban and suburban areas. Able to purchase a home for the first time, many of this generation left the culture they had grown up in for a more "civilized" existence. This shift removed an entire generation out of the folk cultures of the United States and has produced a more homogenized "American" culture, one that is more law abiding, more subservient to the government, and much less likely to follow in the footsteps of generations of moonshiners we saw before the war. This is changing, though, as more people look to their folk ancestry to try and connect with the past, change the future, and live a life they feel has more purpose.

Over the past twenty years, many states and the federal government have loosened restrictions surrounding small distillers. Although it is still a federal crime to distill without a license in the United States, the removal of licensing restrictions has allowed a new wave of distillers to legally enter the marketplace. Some states, such as Missouri, have even legalized home distilling for personal use. The old-time illegal moonshiners, who are mostly dying out, gave way to a more urban, homebrewing public. These distillers—learning their craft on their stove—began to experiment. Moonshine has helped many of these small distilleries come into the marketplace. Because it does not need to be aged, a small, craft, micro-distiller can produce a moonshine and get it to market very quickly, allowing many small distilleries to earn some cash while aging their bourbon or other products. Just like during the pre-Prohibition era, these products can vary widely, depending on the producer, equipment, types of grain used, or even their philosophy.

The trend in commercial moonshine today is to produce a strong, barely sippable product known more for its fire than its taste. Modern underground Appalachian moonshiners are appalled at the taste of most commercial moonshines and corn whiskeys: little to no flavor, hard to drink, and even the novelty of the bottles is not seen as genuine. They do like the trend, though; because more people are trying commercial moonshine they have a larger customer base than ever before. Moonshiners feel once they can get someone to try theirs compared to a commercial product, they will get them hooked on a higher quality, craft-made product, and being illegal gives the customer a sense of danger!

Many commercially-produced moonshines are grain-neutral spirits purchased from a large ethanol producer, cut with distilled water to proof, and then bottled. Many of these taste like a bad vodka or pure grain spirit compared to a true corn whiskey. Others distill a corn whiskey—80% or higher corn mash—from their own mash and copy what is the current reigning flavor profile: hot up front with high esters, crisp and clean, without a real finish or flavor. Many of these have a vodka taste without much of a corn flavor. Others try to recreate what they think was produced in the Appalachian Mountains prior to Prohibition. Still others learned the art and skill from their family in the Appalachian Mountains and became the first to "go legit" with their processes and recipes. These have a smooth front end with a heavy corn flavor tail that is flavorful and distinctive. Each of these small producers has a unique product, as they are not copying the major trend and creating a product using their century-old recipe and process. The farm distillery is also making a comeback. Once numbering in the thousands, a handful of farm distilleries are taking tradition back by growing their own grains, sourcing other ingredients locally, and creating true terroir, hand-made, craft products.

The history of moonshine is far from over. As more and more craft distilleries and home distillers learn and try to pass on the traditions of their families, more consumers fall in love with it. We are seeing city and country folk alike trying and experimenting with traditional moonshine like never before. In most cities around the country you can order specialty drinks produced with legal moonshine. At the illegal speakeasy next door you can try drinks made with illegal moonshine.

That being said, alcohol is a drug and should be treated as such. Please drink and use alcohol responsibly. Please contact Alcoholics Anonymous if you think you are, or may possibly be, an alcoholic. Everyone needs help sometimes. Do not judge.

This book is not meant to be an encyclopedia, serious reference, or anything resembling a how-to. This book, although informative, is full of myths, half-truths, and outright misrepresentations that have been handed down from past generations. In the world of whiskey and moonshine, the story is as important as the product. Heck, modern marketing came out of the alcohol industry. As a result, most products' stories and related histories are at most half-truths or downright lies. Because we are talking about historical uses for moonshine, many of these stories and myths are included. They are interesting, humorous, and sometimes downright dumb, but usually funny. We will try to let you know the difference.

To make reading this book easier, any time someone wished to remain anonymous I have referred to them as my "grandmother" or "grandfather." In real life, I never referred to either of them that way and always called them "mamaw" and "papaw." This way, I can let you know the source was more than likely a person that wished to remain anonymous.

Read at your own risk. The authors are not responsible for anyone attempting to use any of the listed uses and, in fact, we ask that you do not try these at home (or away from home)—ever! Additionally, always consult your doctor about medical issues, your lawyer about legal issues, your dentist about dental issues, your farmer about food issues, your preacher about spiritual issues, your mother about cultural issues, and your dad for everything else. We are not your parents and do not want to be. In the case of the end of the world, you are on your own.

Rolling hills and the main driveway to the Distillery, Shawnee Bend Farms, Union, Missouri. This is the only path into the Distillery.

Chapter Two

Social Skills

Some of the oldest, and arguably the most important, uses for moonshine are those that involve social applications. Moonshine—and alcohol in general—has not only been used for centuries in our society, but also helped to form our society. Society is a fickle beast and booze can calm it. Some of the following uses deal with high society, but some are from the common man. All of them are useful in one way or another.

Conflict Resolver

Alcohol has been used for centuries to ease tension and resolve conflict; just a couple glasses and most conflict is gone. But be careful, as too much alcohol and a new conflict can emerge.

Conflict Starter

If someone drinks a half bottle or more, they will either pass out or start a fight. Guaranteed. If they don't pass out, there will be hell to pay. They may not be the best fighter, or the most coordinated, but it should be a good show at the very least.

Coulter & Payne Farm Distillery. The Still House is the brown building on the right, the Barrel house is the Barn, and the Workshop and Shipping buildings are next to the silver grain bin. Shawnee Bend Farms, Union, Missouri.

Creativity Enhancer

A couple shots of moonshine can grease the wheels and get the brain around mental roadblocks. Be careful not to overdo it, though. A drunk's ramblings, although funny, are not usually the works of art they thought at the time. A case in point: I wrote this whole section after a few pulls off the bottle. Others, though, can create incredible works of art and pieces of literature that survive long after the buzz does.

Entertainment

Open a couple bottles of 'shine. Pass around some glasses and sit back and watch the festivities. We've all done it. Sometimes we are the entertainment and sometimes we are the audience.

Friend Maker

Has anyone ever not been able to make a friend after a glass of moonshine? I think not. Pour a glass and learn all about your new friend.

> "MY OWN EXPERIENCE HAS BEEN THAT THE TOOLS I NEED FOR MY TRADE ARE PAPER, TOBACCO, FOOD, AND A LITTLE WHISKY."
> — William Faulkner, AMERICAN AUTHOR

Inhibition Remover

Related to liquid courage, a couple glasses are good for letting your hair down and giving anyone the courage to talk to that special someone. Many a hookup has resulted from the removal of inhibitions.

Mind Eraser

Everything is a matter of degree. If you drink too much, you will lose all memory of the night's festivities. If you do this too often, you may want to rethink your lifestyle.

Romance

Need some help getting your special lady ready for love? Or at least getting both of you able to relax and enjoy each other? A few glasses of shine and just a little charm and you are on your way to starting a relationship. Then again, it may backfire.

Mountain view and Parksville Lake, Tennessee.

Anti-Viagra

Again, it is a matter of degree. Where a few glasses will get the engine going, too many and the gears stop working. Hang in there! You may need a few more glasses to erase the embarrassment.

Pain Reduction (or Removal)

You've seen it in the movies and most people will tell you it works. A little alcohol will help you feel no pain or simply help you ignore it. A couple shots and most people feel a little invincible, a little numb, and ready to take on whatever's in front of them.

Liquid Courage

For some, a little loosening of the inhibitions and feelings of invincibility can go a long way. It has been called liquid courage, but really, in most cases it's just a way to get out of your own way. Whether it is talking to that intimidating girl—or any girl—or giving you the courage to do the impossible, the whiskey industry has been in the "results" business for a long time.

Pasture and a hay field at Shawnee Bend Farms, Union, Missouri

— Chapter Three —
Survival Skills (End of the World Stuff)

In case of a global economic collapse, revolution, zombie uprising, or other calamity, our daily lives will change dramatically. Are we ready for such an undertaking? Some people think they are, while others haven't given it much thought. In any case, we thought we would show you some of the things that moonshine would be good for in such a situation. We have been told for years that all we really need to survive in this world is food, water, and shelter. This is true. However, are those things always easy to acquire?

Barter/Currency

Regardless of the state of the world, there are always those that will trade and barter to avoid spending cash. Believe it or not, booze is a great item to trade. Need to get by that crazy hermit guarding the road? Slip him a bottle of 'shine. You'll be glad you've got a few bottles if aliens or zombies attack, the economy collapses, or civilization falls. You will be even better off if you can make your own and produce a steady supply. You'll be able to keep ruffians at bay and get in good with your new overlord. Win-win.

Crop Saver

Prior to Prohibition, there were literally thousands of farm distilleries in the United States. Bottles of booze are easier to carry than unprocessed grain and when crops did poorly, farmers could still have something to sell. As long as the grain produced something with starch or sugar you could produce booze. In our post-apocalyptic world, if you have a hard time growing your grain you can still get something out of it. Even if the kids won't eat your run-down looking corn or pest-infested wheat, you can protect the family by using it to make booze that you can sell or trade.

Explosives

By its very nature alcohol is fuel. Alcohol is used in a multitude of compounds used to explode or propel things. For example, rocket fuel was traditionally alcohol based. I am not going to tell you how to make an explosive, since I've worked very hard to keep the feds away, but a good source of alcohol would be very useful during a zombie attack.

Fire Starter

Alcohol, including 'shine, is an excellent fire starter. One of the more important skills in a post-apocalyptic world is fire starting. Fires are good for signaling, heat, cooking, interrogation, making brands, and sterilizing instruments. To make a good one use dry wood, starting with a kindling base and topped off with larger pieces. Alcohol is good to get the fire started, especially on the smaller pieces of kindling. Pour your 'shine on your kindling and let it soak in. If you have plenty, you can pour it on the larger pieces of wood, too. You want it to dry and burn the wood, not just burn off the top. Don't spill it on you and then light the fire, though; we want to start a fire, not set you on fire.

Opposite: "Dolly" the still and mason jars
filled with corn whiskey after a proofing run.

Molotov Cocktails

These little inventions have been around for a while and have gotten plenty of people into trouble with authorities. While I do not recommend doing this in today's society, in the case of a zombie apocalypse, they will come in handy. Simply stuff a fuse (cloth or another slow-burning substance) into a bottle of 'shine, light it, and throw. The alcohol will spread around and the fire will jump from drop to drop. You will want to use something 100 proof or more to ensure the fire will keep lit and do its thing.

Torches

If the world loses power, or if we are without an economy for an extended period of time, torches are going to make a big comeback. They are mobile, allow you to see in the dark, and can be used to set things on fire. The easiest way to make one is to soak a piece of cloth in the 'shine and wrap it around a stick. The length of time it will last will depend on the type of stick and the type of cloth. Another way is to create a homemade oil lamp or similar apparatus and use the 'shine when you run out of oil or other fuel. Still, be careful; alcohol is highly flammable and should only be used when there is nothing else available.

Friend Maker (see #5)

People tend to forget some of their best assets during a crisis are the people around them. No matter what you think, no one can do it entirely on their own. There are always going to be situations that require expertise you don't have. So, if you were going to garner and develop one skill, I would recommend the ability to make friends. With this skill, you can build a network of people to help you through any crisis. Just as it is today, alcohol can help make this easier or help you break that one seemingly "unfriendable" person you may need. A few drinks and almost anyone will open up. If you are friendly, offer some good booze; and if you are hospitable, you're well on your way to securing the next cog in your network.

Disinfecting Field Knife Before Surgery

It is true that fire is a good way to disinfect a field knife, but you never know what the situation may be. If the wood is wet or it's dark out and you do not want to be spotted, it may not be a good time to start a fire. In such cases, your 'shine may be your best bet for a successful lifesaving operation. Keep in mind to give some to your patient; they may need it to deal with the pain from the surgery themselves. Don't let them drink a lot before you start. Alcohol thins the blood and can cause them to bleed out more than necessary. Just give them enough to ease the pain and calm the nerves.

"A DIPLOMAT'S LIFE IS MADE UP OF THREE INGREDIENTS: PROTOCOL, GERITOL, AND ALCOHOL."
~ Adlai E. Stevenson, II, US AMBASSADOR TO THE U.N.

Truth Serum

People like to talk, especially when they have been drinking. If you play your cards right, you can find out just about anything you want after a few drinks of 'shine. Don't push the questions, though; wait until they start offering up secrets or embarrassing information. Then you know you have them. Keep them drinking and they will forget what they told you. Get them to drink enough and they will forget they even talked to you. My grandmother swore by this and many people in the family still use 'shine as a way to find out what really happened in almost any situation. At least they would get the version the person in question believed happened.

Water Purifier

Alcohol will kill a lot of germs—not all, mind you, but a lot. Alcohol should also only be used as a water purifier for an unknown source as a last resort. Find a clean water source, a water purification system, or distill the water instead if you are able. If your water is clean and it is going to be stored for a while, a little 'shine in your canteen or tank with your water will reduce potential contamination and increase the shelf life of your stores.

Water Replacement

Along the same lines, if your water source is contaminated you may be better off just drinking the 'shine. Alcohol will only kill so much and it will not take out particulates or junk in the water. Keep in mind alcohol dehydrates, so don't overdo it. Just take enough to wet the palate and take the edge off until you can find a good source of clean water.

Immobilizing Your Enemies

This one is my favorite. It requires patience and insight into human nature. The easiest but sloppiest way is to send a good amount of booze to your enemies' camp and wait for the bulk of them to start drinking. If you have an idea about the type or personalities of the group you can get the booze into the hands of someone who will help—consciously or inadvertently—spread it around to the members of the group. Meanwhile, you give them the impression that your group is not a threat and you have retreated for the night. Once they are incapacitated you can attack or make your getaway.

Mountain view in East Tennessee near one of the family homesteads.

Chapter Four

Home Use

As Americans, we spend billions of dollars each year on a multitude of cleaning products. We have separate products for cleaning counters, windows, grease, toilets, bathtubs, cars, and so on. We are told that we need such and such product to do the job. As a result, our homes are filled with crates and crates of cleaning, paint, fuel, and related products. What if you could limit the amount of products you were purchasing by relying on one that does all, or at least many of these tasks. There are two products that we can't live without: vinegar, because of its multitude of uses; and 'shine, for the same reason. You should consider keeping both on hand in case of emergencies. Please, use at your own risk!

Backwoods Sanitizer/Deodorizer

Who doesn't like the smell of moonshine? An easy way to freshen up a room is to spray a mixture of water and 'shine. I prefer a mixture of six parts water to one part 'shine. Put it in a spray bottle and you're ready to go. Keep in mind that too high a mixture of alcohol and you will be spraying a flammable mist on your furniture and drapes. You just want the smell, not a firestarter. Also, if you spray it with too much 'shine you could leave spots on your furniture!

Cleaning Glass

'Shine is good for cleaning glass, among other things; the alcohol evaporates, leaving the glass clean. Use a mixture of equal parts water and 'shine for cleaning dust and grease off of glass. If the grease is heavy—like on a light fixture in the kitchen—up the amount of 'shine. Make sure the light is off, though. Please.

Cleaning Pipes and Ashtrays

High-strength 'shine is great for cleaning smoking pipes and removing tar buildup. Be careful on wood pipes, though; the booze may eat through some varnishes and could dry out the wood or plastic, leaving it looking old and worn out. Works great on glass, metal, porcelain, ceramic, and other tough materials.

Grease Remover

A high-proof 'shine is perfect for removing most grease buildup. Remove any easily removed grease first, then apply the 'shine. It is easier if you can soak the dirty area before wiping it clean. Wiping it on and keeping it wet is difficult; it tends to evaporate and leave your area dirty.

Hand Sanitizer

'Shine is a good hand sanitizer in a pinch. Rubbing a 70% alcohol sanitizer for a minute or longer will kill almost 99% of microbes. Keep in mind the alcohol will dry out your hands, though, so don't use it all the time, or at least moisturize afterward. And do not use it when you are getting into a car to drive. Saying "No officer, I wasn't drinking. I was washing my hands" probably won't fly.

Window Cleaner

Use a mixture of three parts water and one part 'shine to clean your windows; the alcohol will evaporate and leave them streak free.

Herbicide

Straight 'shine is a great weed killer. You can probably get away with a mixture of equal parts water and 'shine. If it doesn't kill the weeds right away re-apply later. Keep in mind it will probably kill your plants, too. Just be selective where you spray or pour.

Home Disinfectant

Getting rid of germs is a mainstay of modern America. How better to do it than using America's homegrown spirit? Take a mixture of one part water to two parts moonshine and use it to wipe down counters or cabinets. Do not use it on wood, varnish, or other painted objects; your family may not like the new look of their furniture if your 'shine mixture is too strong!

Opposite: An old truck parked at an overlook on the Cherohala Skyway in East Tennessee.

Increasing Horsepower in Small Engines

Modern-day vehicles run off of anywhere from 1% to 10% ethanol fuel. Other vehicles are formulated for higher ethanol content. Regardless, small engines can handle a little bit of 'shine without much to do. A little bit of the additive to your basic small engine and you will get an increase in horsepower, but be careful not to do it too often or add too much, as the engine will run hot and you could ruin it altogether. As my grandfather would say, "It thins out the mix."

Jewelry Cleaner

Soak your jewelry in some 'shine and prepare to have it as clean as when it was new! Use a 100% solution of moonshine, soak for a while, and scrub with a brush to finish the job.

Metal Cleaner/Equipment Cleaner

Straight moonshine is great for cleaning metal and even for cleaning grease and grime off equipment. Make sure the equipment is turned off so you don't accidently catch the 'shine on fire or short out electrical wiring. Be careful on paint, too! Depending on the type of paint and the strength of the moonshine, you could be setting yourself up for repainting your equipment!

"TOO MUCH OF ANYTHING IS BAD, BUT TOO MUCH GOOD WHISKEY IS BARELY ENOUGH."

—*Mark Twain,* AMERICAN HUMORIST

Mildew Remover

A straight moonshine mix will clean and remove most mildew off shower tiles and tile floors. Be careful around caulk; some caulks will be ruined by alcohol, so be prepared to replace it if you damage it while cleaning the mildew.

Nail Polish Remover

Not that you want to do this all the time, but strong moonshine makes it easy to clean off nail polish. Be careful, as strong moonshine can dry out your hands, leading to cracked skin. If you want to keep your hands looking great, you may want to find another solution.

Pesticide

Mix some moonshine with equal parts water and you have created a simple pesticide. It may take a few applications for some areas, but you will eventually either kill what you are spraying or the bugs will avoid the area. I have noticed a few bugs that don't react to the mix, but most will eventually.

Head Brewer Matthew Schimmel and Distiller Cole Uphouse working on "Bender," a 30-gallon, hybrid column still at Coulter & Payne Farm Distillery.

Antifreeze

#38

If you have ever tried to keep water buckets or rain barrels from freezing during Winter try a cup or two of moonshine. Alcohol lowers the freezing point of water and it is safer for pets and critters, and usually cheaper than commercial antifreeze. Commercial antifreeze is a poison and you definitely do not want to leave it out and open to animals. And by only using a cup or two of shine, you're not going to get the local critters drunk.

Shower Cleaner

#39

Every six months I soak our shower head in full-strength moonshine to break up calcium deposits and remove other gunk that may have built up. Be careful not to get the moonshine on your seals, as the alcohol will dry out most rubber and plastic ones, causing a leak!

Stain Remover

#40

Moonshine will remove a lot of stains, particularly oil-based stains. Continue to use water to get out dirt, but for nasty stains, try a little moonshine. I do not recommend using it without testing it on a hidden spot first; it may remove the dye in your clothing, leaving you with a bigger issue than the stain!

Opposite: A "Parrot" letting moonshine run off the still.

Varnish Remover

Remember #31? I have found moonshine is great for removing most types of varnish and paints. I have a counter with a good-sized section of unvarnished wood that used to be nice and pretty. Live and learn! Let full-strength 'shine sit on the intended area for a while, then wipe up your varnish. Depending on the stain you may also be able to clean stain off.

Paint Remover or Thinner

As with varnish remover, 'shine can be a great and inexpensive paint remover. Test on a hidden spot first to make sure it will work on your particular paint. Also, make sure to keep the moonshine off areas that you don't want cleaned. If you have paint that is too thick, you can also add a little 'shine to thin it out. It works great for polyurethane-based paint.

Wood Stripper

It will take longer to use moonshine for stripping wood, but it will do the job. You'll need to soak the pieces and use a lot of elbow grease to get all the paint and primer off. It may be worth your time using a commercial stripper.

Chapter Five

"Medical" Uses

This is one of the most fun and interesting sections we worked on. Most of these uses are from our family and friends, either in the Appalachian regions of Northern Georgia and Eastern Tennessee or the Ozark region in Missouri. We wanted to showcase some of these uses for moonshine and let the world know how moonshine has been used by our particular culture. We "Mountain Folk" are a superstitious bunch. We will do weird things like bury our hair to ward off headaches, keep shoes upside down at night to help alleviate ailments, and spit on our babies to bring them good luck. Modern folk—especially city folk—have a hard time understanding these superstitions. I even have a hard time understanding them most of the time. Even so, they have shaped our culture and came about for real reasons, even if we don't recognize those reasons today. Our interest in them is not to ridicule or even challenge them; we only want to highlight some of these beliefs. We will not get into many of these in this book, but from time to time something will pop up.

As we have stated before, we are *not* doctors! The following uses are more of a historical review of what alcohol has been used for and not a suggestion to use it to replace adequate medical care. Disclaimer: Read at your own risk. Additionally, always consult with your doctor about medical issues, your lawyer about legal issues, your dentist about tooth issues, your farmer about food issues, your preacher about spiritual issues, your mother about cultural issues, and your dad for everything else. We are not your parents and do not want to be.

Antiseptic

Alcohol can help kill microbes, including most viruses and bacteria. Antiseptics are good to help stop infection and sepsis. Although we suggest you use medical-grade alcohol for this, in a pinch some 'shine will help. My grandmother still keeps a jar of 'shine in the medicine cabinet for emergency use.

Blood Thinner

Alcohol is a blood thinner. I am not quite sure how this knowledge is useful to the everyday person as a use, but it is useful to know that if you have been drinking, your blood will clot slower. This means that it will not clot as easily and you could bleed more than you need to. Get medical attention if you are really drunk (or not) and bleeding profusely! Seriously!

Cold Prevention

My grandmother, as did so many others, swore that a "snort" of 'shine each day would keep colds away. She may have been on to something. Anytime a "snort" of moonshine was used, it was usually pulled out of a jug grandmother had used for an infusion of rock candy, moonshine, and spearmint. When she used it for colds she would make a tea and add some honey and a shot from the jug.

"WELL, BETWEEN SCOTCH AND NOTHIN', I SUPPOSE I'D TAKE SCOTCH. IT'S THE NEAREST THING TO GOOD MOONSHINE I CAN FIND."

~William Faulkner, AUTHOR

Cold Remedy

If someone had a cold my grandmother would step up the cure. She would take a "snort" of 'shine, add some ground ginger and ground red pepper, and add it to tea sweetened with honey. If she had it, she would also add lemon juice.

Cough Remedy

My grandmother may have been on to something. She would take a "snort" of 'shine in a cup of green tea and make it thick with honey for coughs. It could be the honey, but the 'shine helps it go down.

Flu Prevention

My grandmother … 'shine had a lot of uses in the mountains. Mix "a little tea, honey, and a 'snort' of shine, and the flu you would not find."

Mouthwash

Most commercial mouthwashes have a little alcohol in them, and 'shine is an antiseptic and will kill most microbes. Mix a shot of 'shine in a cup of water, add some peppermint, and you've got a basic mouthwash. You can adjust the amount of booze to make it a little stronger or weaker. My grandfather is rumored to have said that during "the war" (I'm not sure which one), 'shine was the only thing that kept his teeth from rotting out. I am pretty sure he was either just kidding or he was rationalizing his drinking problem, but it makes for a good story either way.

Pain Reliever

My grandfather would take a "snort" of 'shine for a headache or other pains. He was thought to have had headaches a lot. I mean a *lot*. He may have had a drinking problem.

Sedation

I'm not sure what was really meant by this, but I think we're talking about calming people down. It works with some people, but with others it seems to liven them up. Maybe it is a matter of the amount of the prescription or the frequency.

Keeping Husbands Quiet

Similar to sedation, who would argue with me that giving a man a glass of 'shine and telling him to go sit in his man cave wouldn't shut him up? My grandmother would give my grandfather a couple drinks to shut him up and get him to do whatever she wanted, or to get out of trouble for doing something he didn't like. I can't say things are any different today in some families.

Field corn about a month after planting. We plant in early June and harvest before October.

Settling Upset Stomach

Again, a "snort" of 'shine in a glass of tea and honey was used extensively to settle the stomach.

Sweating Out the Flu

Modern-day medicines swear by prescriptions of lots of rest, water, and drugs. Mountain people swear by 'shine, tea, honey, and cussin' out doctors. Some things change, but others don't. More people go to doctors now, but they still cuss them up and down and sneak off to have their glass of 'shine, honey, and tea while they get back on their feet.

Tinctures

Tinctures are extracts made using alcohol to pull out the oils and flavors from herbs, vegetables, and other plants. These extracts are used in holistic medicine, mountain medicine, and even modern-day supplements to western medicine. The basic method uses a 40% alcohol product ('shine works well) or higher in a jar and your herb. Shake every few days and within a few weeks, your tincture should be done. I think it works best at 100 proof, so if your moonshine is higher cut it down with some water. My grandmother usually called these "elixirs" and they were commonplace on mantels and in medicine cabinets in East Tennessee.

Tonic for Menstrual Cramps

There are a ton of these recipes on the internet and they focus mainly on diuretics. Gin and tonics are mentioned quite often. Instead of focusing on these, I thought I would pass along one from my grandmother that seems the most interesting. It was meant to be kept in a cabinet so it was ready whenever needed. Make an infusion of Juniper berries, horsetail, peppermint or spearmint, and moonshine in a jar. Let it sit. Add a shot of this to your hot tea as needed. Keep in mind that juniper, horsetail, mint, and tea are all diuretics. Sometimes rock candy was added, as well.

Toothaches

For minor toothaches, my grandmother would rub a little 'shine on the area in question. It will numb the area and reduce the pain. It's not meant for teeth that need pulling or other major dental issues!

Arthritis

Several of our family members used to take a "snort" of moonshine mixed with honey and vinegar to ease the pain of arthritis. Maybe not a cure, but it helped the pain.

Asthma

There are a million asthma remedies out there, and each of them has something that may be worthwhile. My grandmother's is simple, and each year we find out how it may actually have some merit. She used a "snort" of moonshine made from her infusion of rock candy, moonshine, and spearmint that she soaked juniper berries in. When this was done infusing (a few weeks), she would mix that with equal parts local honey (preferably wild honey) and black tea.

Chest Congestion Relief

One of my favorite recipes I found among our family members was an old treatment for chest congestion. They would take a little 'shine in a jar, add enough rock candy to make a syrup, and drink a little every few hours. For the life of me I can't understand why anyone thought it would work, but several old-timers swore by it. With all the other "snorts" being taken all the time, it is a wonder anyone survived!

Male Potency (ED)

For years, people have sworn by the power of 'shine to put a little "spring in their step." This may be true for those that suffer from stress-related ED, as a little 'shine may help them relax to a point where ED is no longer an issue. Moonshine will not, however, be a cure-all for everyone, I am sorry to say.

One of the recipes comes from my grandfather in South Carolina. Some rooster blood, bull's blood, ginseng root, and a shot of 'shine would make any man ready to father more than his fair share of offspring. Animal attributes passing on to humans is a common theme in the mountains. I think the 'shine just made it all go down a little easier.

Colic

Giving babies moonshine is not the safest thing I have heard of, but we mountain people seem to do it quite often. The method used by my grandmother was a little ginseng root mixed with a few drops of moonshine given to the baby in some milk. I am assuming the alcohol helped to calm the baby, but what do I know? Grandpa Mac used to give all the grandkids peppermint schnapps in hot chocolate to get them to go to bed. They always loved Grandpa's hot chocolate! None of the parents knew for a long time!

Croup

I have seen a lot of croup remedies, including one where you hold a baby over a fire of turpentine and moonshine. If my family did this they didn't mention it. My grandmother's remedy was a "snort" of shine with some ginger mixed with honey, vinegar, and green tea.

Cure-Alls

This first one has been mentioned several times in passing; 'shine, tea, rock candy, mint, and honey are the base for many of the potions used in my family. Some add other herbs from time to time, such as juniper, ginseng root, and mint. The base to many of the elixirs was rock candy, spearmint, and 'shine that was infused in a jug or jar and added to tea and honey at the time of consumption.

Another similar family concoction uses 'shine, but adds ginseng or ginseng tea as the base, instead of black tea. Ginseng is thought to improve the immune system. I think I would combine them all, but what do I know? I'm just a "young 'un!"

Dysentery

This is one of the weirdest remedies we have in the family. To be fair, I have seen it elsewhere, but that doesn't make it any less strange. My grandmother would take a "snort" out of her jug, put it into a cup, and set it on fire. When it goes out, drink it all up.

"HAPPINESS IS HAVING A RARE STEAK, A BOTTLE OF WHISKY, AND A DOG TO EAT THE RARE STEAK."

— *Johnny Carson*, HOST OF *LATE NIGHT WITH JOHNNY CARSON*

Gall Bladder Trouble

According to my grandmother, a "snort" of 'shine with the root of "Old Man's Beard" (White Fringetree) is supposed to help your gall bladder produce more bile, which will help clean out your gall bladder.

Headaches

My grandmother would prescribe for headaches a "snort" of 'shine from the jug mixed with a cup of strong black tea or a cup of coffee sweetened with honey. I still do this today and it usually works.

Pneumonia

There seem to be a lot of remedies for respiratory illness that involve moonshine. Maybe it's because that was one of the leading causes of death in the backwoods. My grandmother would make a tea concoction using a "snort" of 'shine, ginger, red pepper, ginseng, vinegar, and honey and mix in a black tea. It is not as bad as it sounds and maybe it works!

Rheumatism

My grandmother would prepare an elixir of a "snort" of 'shine mixed with ginseng, wild cherry bark, honey, and vinegar that was to be drunk a couple times each day to alleviate the pains of rheumatism.

Sore Throat

Start with a "snort" of 'shine from the jug infused with spearmint and rock candy. Mix it with an herbal tea sweetened with honey and you have got one of the best drinks for a sore throat. Best if served hot, or you can gargle the drink once it has cooled down.

Spider Bites

As an old Appalachian folk remedy for spider bites, my grandmother would prescribe a "snort" of 'shine and a salve made from moonshine, mint, and corn starch. Supposedly, the salve would draw up the venom and the 'shine would help the body fight off the effects. We mostly know today that people that are bitten would probably survive without the cure.

Whooping Cough Cure

I do not recommend relying on this as a "cure," but a "snort" of 'shine was considered to be a "cure" of whooping cough in the mountains. I am not sure if it actually worked, and I'd bet that it only served to calm the cough for a while. Think of it as a way to treat the symptom instead of the disease.

Opposite: Pasture at Shawnee Bend Farms, Union, Missouri.

#74

Snake Bites

In the mountains—similar to spider bites—people bitten by snakes were given a salve and some 'shine or other alcohol. This is probably not the safest or smartest method of dealing with snake bites. It was thought the alcohol thinned the blood and fought off the venom. The salve was used to pull out the venom after you had sucked out the majority of it. The oral prescription was a large amount of alcohol! We know today the only method proven to fight venom is the anti-venom for that particular snake. Most people that survived after drinking a lot of alcohol probably would have survived anyway. It is even more likely some of the people that did not survive would have if it hadn't been for the large dose of 'shine.

Because of the confusion and myths around snake bites, I am going to give the approved first aid procedures. Most snake bites are from non-poisonous snakes. According to the

Center for Disease Control, between 7,000 and 8,000 people are bitten by poisonous snakes each year. Of these, only five are fatal. If bitten, make sure the patient is safe from further bites from the snake and call 911. Once safe from danger, keep the patient still. Observe the snake and take note of its markings so the doctors will know what kind of snake it is. Remain calm with the wound below the heart, so the venom doesn't move through the bloodstream quickly. Cover the wound with a loose bandage. Do not cut a bite wound; attempt to suck out the venom; apply a tourniquet, ice, or water; or give the person alcohol or caffeinated drinks. Odds are greatly in their favor that the bite will not result in death, but treat any bite like it is a poisonous one to be safe.

Keeping Evil Spirits at Bay

Everyone needs to have a way to keep evil away. Why not some 'shine? My grandmother would keep a jar of moonshine on the mantel. As it dried out she would refill it, never letting it completely dry up. She said this kept angels in our home (and kept them happy), which kept evil spirits out. The jar was also used to give visitors a "snort" and for coughs and cold prevention.

Chapter Six

Recipes

Any book that lists uses of moonshine must contain a section on recipes and cocktails! The flavor of moonshine can be a great addition to food, and there are many sauces on the market today that use whiskey in one form or another. If you are scared of drinking moonshine straight, a cocktail is the way to go. A good cocktail can help bring out the flavors hiding in your favorite drinks and make you feel great! We have included some of our favorites, along with some that are traditionally used in bars and homes in East Tennessee. We've even included a few we have come up with. This is a great list to help you come up with your own special concoction.

#76

Moonshine BBQ Sauce

Here's a basic recipe for a moonshine bbq sauce. We play with it and adjust it each time until we're happy. Have fun!

Ingredients:
1oz. Salted Butter
2oz. Minced Onion
1½ Cups Moonshine
½ cup Hot Water
6 tbsp Beef Base
¼ cup Hot Sauce
½ cup Red Wine Vinegar
¼ cup Worcestershire Sauce
4⅛ Cups Light Brown Sugar
¼ cup Cornstarch
¼ cup Cold Water

Directions:
In a pan, melt the butter over medium-high heat and add the onion. Sauté for 2 minutes. Add moonshine around the pan to deglaze. Reduce liquid by half (50%). In a mixing bowl mix water, beef base, hot sauce, vinegar, and Worcestershire. Once mixed, add it to the pan. Whisk in brown sugar and bring the sauce to a boil. In a small bowl, whisk cornstarch and water into a slurry. Slowly add to the sauce, whisking constantly. Lower the heat and simmer for 5 minutes. Cool in an ice bath (40 degrees or lower).

"AMERICANS ARE BIG BOYS. YOU CAN TALK THEM INTO ALMOST ANYTHING. JUST SIT WITH THEM FOR HALF AN HOUR OVER A BOTTLE OF WHISKEY AND BE A NICE GUY."

~Nguyen Cao Ky, VIETNAMESE POLITICAL LEADER

Moonshine-Flavored Candy

There are a ton of ways to make candy, and a little bit of 'shine goes a long way. You can add some 'shine to sugar candy, chocolate, cremes, ice cream, and jellied candies without having to adjust the recipe too much. Some will need you to replace water with moonshine, while others will allow you to simply add the moonshine to the batch.

Moonshine Lemon Sauce with Pasta

A very nice and sophisticated sauce to use with pasta. Excellent with lemon chicken and pasta!

Ingredients:
3 tsp Salt
1 lb Pasta
2 large Lemons
¼ cup Moonshine
1 cup Heavy Whipping Cream
¼ tsp Pepper
¼ cup Chopped Basil
½ cup Parmesan Cheese
¼ cup Parmesan Cheese

Directions:

In a large pot bring water to a boil with 3 tsp salt. Cook the pasta for 8–10 minutes. Prepare the lemons: grate the rind of one lemon and reserve. Squeeze the juice of both lemons and reserve. In a medium saucepan heat the moonshine and cream until it thickens. Add the lemon rind and juice to the cream mixture. Stir well. Add in pepper, basil, and ½ cup parmesan cheese. Heat for 1 minute and remove from heat. Drain the pasta and place it in a large pasta bowl. Pour the creamed mixture over it and toss well. Serve with ¼ cup parmesan cheese as topping.

Food Preserving

Preserving food with alcohol is easy and much less difficult to mess up than canning. You can preserve many foods in alcohol, but the best are fruits and berries. After a few months in a jar with some 'shine they become alcoholic treats and the booze takes on the characteristics of the fruit. We will take a variety—apricots, blackberries, blueberries, strawberries, and apples—and put them in a jar with some 'shine. When they've sat for a while, we will make drinks with the 'shine and make desserts with the fruit and berries. The pies are to die for.

Moonshine Jelly

Moonshine jelly today is usually made with white wine, since moonshine was illegal or hard to get. It is an interesting jelly!

Ingredients:
3 cups Moonshine
5¼ cups Sugar
1 box Pectin

Directions:
Put the ingredients in a large pot. Bring the mixture to a rolling boil. While boiling, stir until the liquid clabbers off a spoon. Skim off all the foam. Pour into jars. This will make around 6 pints. Immediately screw on lids and process in a water bath; be careful, the jars will be hot. Leave the jelly there overnight. It may take a few days to set up. Follow basic canning instructions to make sure you have properly canned and sealed the jelly.

Moonshine Dessert Sauce

This sauce is one of the best out there! It is great over desserts and ice cream. I had to work hard to convince Elise to give this one up!

Ingredients:
¼ cup (½ stick) Unsalted Butter
½ cup Sugar
3 tbsp Heavy Cream
2 tbsp Moonshine
A Pinch of Salt

Directions:
Melt the butter in a small saucepan over medium heat. Whisk in the remaining ingredients. Simmer until thickened, whisking often, about three minutes. Cool slightly.

Moonshine Milkshake

Who doesn't like boozy milkshakes? Moonshine makes a great addition to your ice cream flavors. While you're at it, substitute the moonshine for bourbon, rum, or any other distilled spirit for variety!

Ingredients:
¾ cup Milk
¼ tsp Vanilla Bean Paste
1 cup vanilla/vanilla bean ice cream, slightly softened
1 oz Moonshine

Directions:
In a blender, add the milk, vanilla bean paste, and the ice cream and blend until smooth. Add in the moonshine and give a quick pulse. Pour into a glass and enjoy.

Grandma's Cure-all Tonic

Everybody needs a jug of Grandma's Cure-all Tonic! Used for all kinds of ailments, as the base to many elixirs, and to make visitors and friends feel at home. It is a great drink by itself or mixed in other cocktails and concoctions!

Directions:

Use a half-gallon glass jug or glass milk bottle. Pour in one bottle of high-proof (100 or more) moonshine. Add 4–5 sprigs of spearmint or basil. Shake the jar. Add 4 sticks of rock candy. Let the mixture sit for at least 4 days before using. You can add more rock candy or spearmint/basil to flavor to your liking. You can chop or muddle the mint/basil for more flavor, but you will add color to the jar. Put it on your mantel to keep bad spirits away.

On the Rocks

Drinking a good moonshine on the rocks really brings out the corn flavor and smooths out the heat. Once you try it with an Appalachian-style moonshine you will be a convert.

Directions:

Pour about 3 oz of moonshine in a glass. Add about half a glass of chopped ice. Stir and enjoy.

Apple Pie Moonshine

There are a hundred recipes on the internet for apple pie moonshine. It is a great Winter drink and is excellent heated. Here's our favorite, made by my Uncle Pudgie in East Tennessee.

Directions:

... On second thought, he threatened to kill me if I told anyone about his recipe. You're on your own.

Moonshine Lemoncello
(City folk spell it Limoncello)

This is one of our favorites. Nothing is more fun to make or as satisfying on a hot day. If yours isn't the best thing you have ever had, you've either made it incorrectly or you are using the wrong moonshine.

Directions:

First, prepare the moonshine infusion. Pour one bottle of moonshine (preferably 100 proof) in a glass half-gallon milk jug or similar glass container. Peel 10 lemons and put the peels in the jar. Let sit for 3–5 days, until the moonshine is bright yellow.

Second, prepare the lemonade. Take the leftover lemons and squeeze them. Strain out the seeds, but the pulp is good for you!

Then, make a simple syrup by combining 1 cup of sugar and 2 cups of water and boiling it down; this takes about 15 minutes. Cool.

Bottled moonshine and lemonchello.

Add the simple syrup and lemon juice and mix together to make lemonade. Keep it in the fridge until the booze is done infusing.

Finally, combine the lemonade and moonshine infusion. You might want to add water to taste.

Pour in a glass, garnish, and enjoy!

Silky Smooth Reformed Bourbon

A very strong drink, it is surprisingly smooth and complex. Definitely worth a try the next time you want to try a bourbon and moonshine!

Directions:

Add to cocktail shaker 1 oz. Coulter & Payne™ Small Batch Bourbon, 1 oz. 100-proof moonshine, 1 oz. dry vermouth, 1 oz. benedictine, 1 dash spicy bitters, and ice. Shake. Pour into a glass and garnish with a lemon peel.

Grandmother's Hot Toddy

My grandmother would make this when she wasn't too worried about catching a cold and didn't have a cough. She didn't call it a hot toddy, though—she called it a "drink!"

Directions:

Mix in a glass 1 oz. ("snort") of Moonshine, 1 tsp honey, and 1 tsp lemon juice. Garnish with spearmint or basil.

Grandpa's "Cold Remedy"

This one has been in the family for many years. It is a nice, easy drink to make that's great for sitting next to the fire. I have been known to drink this one quite often.

Directions:

Mix together in a glass 1 oz moonshine and 1 oz Grenadine. Garnish with a cherry.

Replacement for Vodka

Believe it or not, a good moonshine can be used as a replacement for vodka. We use ours in most drinks that normally call for vodka. We've used it in margaritas, White Russians, Bloody Marys, and any number of mixed drinks. Remain aware of the proof of the moonshine and do not go overboard! Here are some traditional recipes to help you along (see following)!

Blackberry Cooler

A refreshing drink that is great in warm weather created by Elise for the Coulter & Payne Farm Distillery™.

Directions:

To prepare the glass, rub the rim with a lemon wedge, dip it in sugar, and fill with ice. Add the following ingredients to a blender and blend for 10 seconds: 2 tsp blackberry jam, 1½ oz of 100-proof moonshine, 4 oz of sparkling water; 1½ tsp of simple syrup, ½ tsp chopped basil. Pour into a glass and stir in 6–8 frozen blackberries. Garnish with basil and a lemon twist.

Blackberry Cooler Cocktail

BBQ Bloody Mary

A Southern-style BBQ Bloody Mary created by Elise for the Coulter & Payne Farm Distillery™.

Directions:

Prepare the glass: rub the rim of the glass with a lime wedge and dip the rim of the glass in ¼ tsp Elise's Barbecue Dry Rub (see following).

Mix the following together and chill for 15 minutes: ¾ tsp Elise's Barbecue Dry Rub (see recipe below) and ½ cup vegetable juice.

After chilling, mix with the ingredients below: 1 tsp lime juice, 1 tsp Worcestershire sauce, and 1½ oz 100-proof moonshine. Fill with cracked ice.

Shake vigorously.

Once mixed, pour into a prepared glass. Garnish with a lime wedge and Serve.

Elise's Dry Rub Barbecue Recipe

Mix together:
1 tbsp Chili Powder
1 tsp Dried Granulated Garlic
1 tsp Paprika
1 tsp Kosher Sea Salt
1 tsp Brown Sugar
½ tsp Chopped Oregano
½ tsp Ground Coriander
½ tsp Ground Cumin
½ tsp Ground Sage
½ tsp Granulated Onion
¼ tsp Minced Garlic
¼ tsp Ground Red Pepper
Will make enough for 7–8 drinks.

Coffee Liqueur

This is the best coffee liquor we have ever tasted. It was created by Amanda Snyder for Chris's birthday! Perfect for mixing in cocktails or drinking on the rocks.

Directions:

Add to a glass bottle 3 cups of moonshine, 1 cracked vanilla bean, ½ cup ground coffee.

Make simple syrup: bring 4 cups of water and 4 cups of sugar to a boil, then let cool.

Add the simple syrup to the moonshine bottle and shake.

Store in a cool, dark place for 3 weeks, shaking every other day.

After 3 weeks strain and put in a clean bottle. Enjoy!

Peach Cooler

Another refreshing drink that is a bit sweeter for those hot summer nights. Another Elise creation!

Directions:

To prepare the glass, rub the rim with a lemon wedge, dip in sugar, and fill with ice.

Add the following ingredients to a blender and blend for 10 seconds: 1 tbsp peach jam (or preserves), 1 frozen peach slice, 4 oz ginger ale, and 1½ oz moonshine.

Pour the mixture into the glass and garnish with the frozen peach slice and a sprig of mint.

Moonshine Bloody Mary

A traditional Bloody Mary that is less work than Elise's! It is still great and works well with moonshine.

Directions:

Shake the following ingredients with cracked ice: 1½ oz moonshine, 3 oz tomato juice, ½ oz lemon juice, a dash of Worcestershire, a dash of salt, a dash of pepper, and a dash of horseradish.

Strain the mixture into a glass and serve.

Moonshine Bloody Mary Cocktail

Muddy Moonshine

A twist on a traditional White Russian. It is my favorite drink and stand-by. It's even better if you make your own coffee liqueur to use in it!

Directions:

Put ice in a cup and stir together the following: 1½ oz Irish creme, 1 oz coffee liqueur, and 1 oz moonshine.

Top off with milk or cream and serve.

Wrong side of the Tracks Mint Julep

A traditional Southern specialty using moonshine instead of bourbon. Moonshine has a reputation for being rowdy: born on the wrong side of the tracks!

Directions:

Muddle together in a tall glass 3 sprigs fresh mint, 1 tsp sugar, and 1 tsp water.

Then fill the glass with shaved or crushed ice and add 1 oz moonshine.

Stir until the glass is frosted.

Add ½ oz moonshine.

Garnish with a mint sprig and a straw and serve.

Moonshine Old Fashioned

Another favorite using moonshine instead of whiskey. Very refreshing and highlights your moonshine!

#98

Directions:

Muddle together 1 tsp fine sugar and a dash of bitters, then add 1 oz moonshine and mix/blend well.

Then stir gently while adding 1 oz moonshine and ice cubes;

Finally, add 1–2 Maraschino cherries and garnish with an orange slice.

Poor Man's Manhattan

Moonshine is considered a poor person's substitute for aged whiskey. We do not agree, but we'll take the name!

#99

Directions:

Stir together well with ice cubes the following ingredients: 1½ oz moonshine, a dash of bitters, ½ oz (sweet or dry) vermouth, and a Maraschino cherry (sweet) or lemon twist (dry).

Hand-Making Your Own
Bourbon Whiskey without a Barrel

A good corn whiskey moonshine can be a great base for your own aged whiskey or bourbon. It is an easy process and only requires a few ingredients and a little patience.

Ingredients and Supplies:

One bottle of your favorite moonshine or corn whiskey. We prefer our Coulter & Payne™ Moonshine White Whiskey.

Three to four pint-sized mason jars.

A good-sized piece of American White Oak or a couple small bags of White Oak wood chips. If you'd like a more Scotch-like whiskey, use a bag of wood chips for smoking made out of used Bourbon or Tennessee Whiskey barrels.

Process: To make wood chips, chop off several small pieces (less than an inch square), until you have enough to fill all the mason jars. Place the wood chips on a cooking sheet lined with aluminum foil.

Go outdoors! Toast or smoke the wood chips for about 45 minutes between 250 and 500°F. Keep in mind that each toast range brings out different flavors in the wood: the lower the temp the more the oak flavor will prevail, while the higher the temp, the more other flavors come out. Try different temperatures for different-tasting whiskeys. It is ok if they char! *Warning!* Do not do this indoors as wood tends to smoke as it heats up. You do not want to fill your house with smoke!

After toasting your wood chips, take a small torch (I use a crème brulee torch) and char (burn) the wood on each side until they've got a good, dark char. Let them sit for an hour or so to cool. Fill your mason jars ¾ full with wood chips.

Top off with the moonshine. Sit them on a shelf and shake the jars once per day. It will take anywhere between 2 to 5 days. When it tastes ready, strain through a coffee filter into a clean jar. Pour about 2 inches in the bottom of a glass and add two ice cubes. Enjoy!

Making Your Own Bourbon with a Barrel

This one is a little easier to do, but takes some of the craft and experimentation out of your hands.

Ingredients and Supplies:

Two bottles of your favorite moonshine or corn whiskey. We use our Coulter & Payne™ Moonshine White Whiskey. A 1- or 2-liter bourbon or whiskey barrel; these can be found in our online store through our website at www.coulterandpaynefarmdistillery.com. A 1-liter barrel will take 1¼ bottles to fill. A 2-liter barrel will take 2½ bottles to fill.

Process:

Prep your barrel following the instructions that come with the barrel. Fill your barrel with your favorite moonshine or corn whiskey. Wait. After a couple weeks it will be ready. Taste it every few days to check its progress. These barrels can be used multiple times. Keep in mind that each time you use it, it will take a little longer to age. Enjoy!

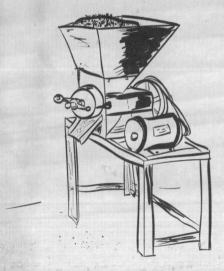

Chapter Seven
The Modern Farm Distillery

What makes a farm distillery? In its simplest form, it is a farm that uses a portion of its crops for the production of alcohol. Before Prohibition, it was much easier for a farm to distill this way. Once stills were regulated tax penalties increased and markets were shut down to these farmers, so farm distilling all but stopped. But, as happens with progress, small farms are now beginning to see the roadblocks diminished. What was once very difficult and expensive is now becoming attainable. The permits are not as difficult to get and the overhead costs of complying with regulations, as well as producing spirits, are getting cheaper. It is now a reasonable venture for a savvy farmer with some marketing and business know-how.

As a farm distillery, you can grow your own ingredients, control the quality, and create an artisanal product. Because you also have another source of income, you do not have to rely solely on the alcohol to make ends meet. It becomes a value-added product, bringing you more income per bushel than just selling the grain. You can also grow specialty crops and make interesting products based on them. This is much more difficult for a city distillery to do, since its operators will have to source the ingredients and work to convince the public that it's worth a try after they have spent the money. Being on a farm also means you have lots of space: space for aging barrels, making product, grinding and malting grain, storing bottles, and so forth. It also means you can probably get rid of your spent grain fairly easily—either to yourself or a neighbor for animal feed.

Farm distilleries have no need to fake their production. They don't need to buy other people's products and just bottle them or use someone else's ingredients and skip making their products; it is seen as disingenuous, fake, and untrustworthy. You are more likely to see the words "distilled by" on the label of a true farm distillery's product. This term has a specific meaning under the law in the United States. Many distilleries use terms like "bottled by," "produced by," "handcrafted by," and so on to show you they are legit. These are just fine to use, and may actually be true, but if they don't include the words "distilled by" then they did not actually make the product. The other words are just marketing terms, with no real meaning under the law. "Distilled by" means that *this* distillery ran their product through their own still to produce the product in the bottle. If it doesn't have this, they didn't. Simple as that.

Supporting a farm distillery is a great way to support farming, your neighbors, and your community. Every farm is intrinsically tied to its community and will rarely do anything to jeopardize their relationships. Farmers work with each other, share seed and equipment, and give to their communities when they can. They want to create great products that support their families without preying on others. When they screw up, they don't just answer to their shareholders or board members; they answer to the preacher down the road, their great aunt who helped raise them, and the children that look up to them, not to mention their fellow farmers and small business people. They have a lot riding on their image and trustworthiness. If they betray that trust, they are as good as dead.

Ask a true farm distiller how they make their products and they will tell you, from who they use for barrels and yeast to how their process formed and what they are planning in the future—they're an open book. I'll tell you just about everything, except the temperatures I distill off at. I've got to keep something secret!

Vanilla-infused moonshine after a couple weeks.

— Chapter Eight —
Coulter & Payne Farm Distillery

Our distillery is a small, craft, micro-distillery in Union, Missouri, that focuses on environmental sustainability, corporate responsibility, our family, and our community. Our family includes our employees. After one year of service every employee has the opportunity to become a shareholder and board member. We believe that our employees, customers, and neighbors are part of our family and we work hard to treat them that way.

One of only a handful of distilleries in the United States that actually grow their own grain, we at Coulter & Payne Farm Distillery use our family farm, Shawnee Bend Farms, to grow only non-GMO grains and other ingredients to use in our products. We do not use pesticides or herbicides, practice environmentally friendly farming practices, and provide non-GMO grain to other local distilleries and farmers that can't grow it themselves. We do everything ourselves, from designing our labels, running our social media, and growing our grains to hand-labeling our bottles. We also work to re-use, recycle, and repurpose everything we can to minimize our impact, including using rainwater to cool the stills in a one of-a-kind, repurposed cooling system; recycling 100% of all paper, metal, and plastic wastes; sending our spent grain to our neighbors and local farmers for free to use as feed; and using only locally sourced materials and supplies. Our labels, bottles, boxes, printed materials, barrels, and wood materials are all sourced within seventy-five miles of the farm when it can't be provided by the farm. We are carbon neutral and are working on installing our first solar power system. Nothing is wasted and everything is hand-made. "Changing the World for the Better, One Drink at a Time."

Inside the Coulter & Payne Farm Distillery, Union, Missouri.

Head Brewer Matt Schimmel and Distiller Cole Uphouse preparing corn for cooking and mashing at the Distillery.

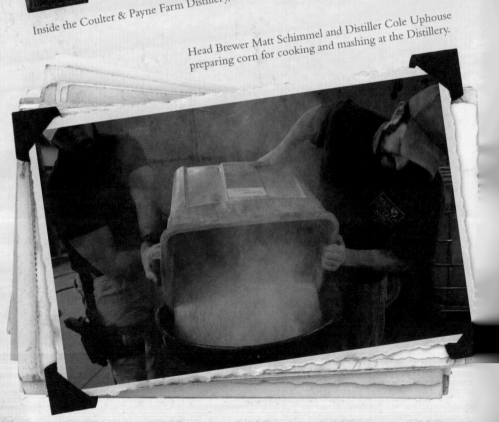

Preparing for a head cut of moonshine. Head cuts are how small distilleries remove unwanted flavors to smooth out and balance the flavor profile of their final products.

Collecting heads prior to taking the head cut on a moonshine run.

Tasting heads to decide where to make the head cut.

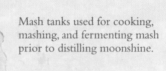
Mash tanks used for cooking, mashing, and fermenting mash prior to distilling moonshine.

Thermometer and sight glass on "Flexo," a 30-gallon, hybrid column still at Coulter & Payne Farm Distillery.

Cooking corn to prepare for mashing and fermentation.

Chris and Cole pouring mash into "Flexo,"
preparing for a distillation run of moonshine.

Chris sifting some corn mash before
a test batch run of moonshine.

"Bender" and "Flexo" running an overnight moonshine run.

Custom handmade keg still, Franklin County, Missouri.

Non-GMO corn cob, or more aptly named "Pre-Whiskey."

Homemade coffee pot still,
St. Charles County, Missouri.

Moonshine in a mason jar.

"TELL ME WHAT BRAND OF WHISKEY THAT GRANT DRINKS. I WOULD LIKE TO SEND A BARREL OF IT TO MY OTHER GENERALS."

~ Abraham Lincoln, 16TH US PRESIDENT

Pulling some corn out of the grain bin prior to grinding.

BUTLER

Cooked corn ready for mashing and fermentation.

Stirring mash during cooking.

Cleaning the floors at the Distillery. Cooking corn is a messy business.

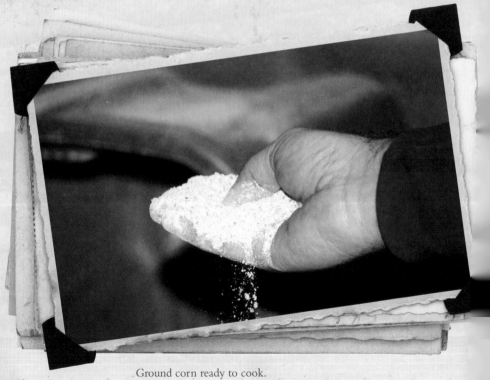

Ground corn ready to cook.

Corn whiskey mash ready for a grain-in beerstripping run.

Mason jars of moonshine sitting in front of "Dolly" the still.

Jars of 'shine waiting for a head cut.

Mash cooker during a cook.

Head Brewer Matt Schimmel dumping corn into "Dolly" to do a test batch cook.

Mason jars lined up, waiting for a head cut.

Jars of corn, spring water, and moonshine.

Corn whiskey running off the still.

Field-dried Yellow #2 corn prior to harvest.

Vanilla bean soaking in moonshine. It will take a
few weeks to pull out the flavor of the vanilla bean.

Moonshine Martini. Just replace vodka with moonshine.

"Dolly" the still next to three mash cookers.
The mash cookers are flame heated with propane.

"A WOMAN DROVE ME TO DRINK AND I DIDN'T HAVE THE DECENCY TO THANK HER."
—*W. C. Fields*, AMERICAN COMIC AND ACTOR

Called a "parrot," this lets a distiller "proof" the distillate as it comes off the still. The parrot holds a hydrometer, constantly letting the distiller know what the current proof is.

Catching moonshine during a late night distillation run. During the summer, it is easier to do runs at night, when it's cooler.

Bottling and labeling a batch of moonshine corn whiskey. We hand-bottle and label each batch prior to sale. Pictured are Amanda Snyder, Chris Burnette, and Cole Uphouse.

Shawnee Bend Farms with Coulter & Payne Farm Distillery.

Chris checking out "Dolly" before a run. Dolly is an electric powered bain marie style hybrid column still from Artisan Still Design.

Every building in a distillery must be labeled by law.

COULTER & PAYNE FARM DISTILLERY

DSP-MO-20006

BLDG 4 WORK SHOP

We did ours the old-fashioned way.

The Distillery's Barrel House at Shawnee Bend Farms, Union, Missouri.
Our son's fort is in the background.

—— About the Authors ——

Chris Burnette, President, Coulter & Payne Farm Distillery, CEO Shawnee Bend Farms

Chris is an avid whiskey maker and drinker, guitar player, environmentalist, attorney, family man, and advocate of the Oxford comma. He currently serves as the President and Head Distiller at the Coulter & Payne Farm Distillery. Chris is responsible for all aspects of the company, including coming up with all the distillery's products, their recipes, and the final product. He is also sought out by other commercial distillers for insight and training in the science and art of

Co-author Chris Burnette, President and Head Distiller at Coulter & Payne Farm Distillery, inspects corn prior to field drying and harvest.

distilling and serves as a sales rep for an international still manufacturer. He currently consults with dozens of distilleries on production issues, grain sourcing, legal compliance, and business start-up. He serves as CEO of Shawnee Bend Farms in Union, Missouri, and is a board member of the Tuli and Burnette Spirits Company, Ltd. in Nagpur, India, where he helps guide a small distilling company carving a niche for itself making American-style spirits for Indian consumers.

He holds a bachelor's degree in American political studies with a concentration in environmental law and policy from Northern Arizona University, a master of arts degree in nonprofit administration with a concentration in public management from Lindenwood University, and a juris doctor degree with a concentration in urban development, land use, and environmental law from Saint Louis University School of Law. He currently serves on the board of the Missouri Coalition for the Environmental and serves as either an advisor or board member to other farm-based nonprofits.

Chris's family has been in the United States since Jamestown Colony (1628–1630) and distilling has been a part of that tradition since the beginning. Having grown up in East Tennessee, moonshine was more than a novelty; it was a constant reminder of the family's origins. The first Burnette was distilling in Scotland as early as the 1500s, and other sides of his family began shortly after. Another line of his family had the first operating still in Gatlinburg, Tennessee, possibly in East Tennessee. Other family members include several men arrested for bootlegging during Prohibition and after, and one great-uncle died in prison after being caught for shining. The rest of his moonshining family has passed on, but not before Chris learned the family tradition. Being the first to pay taxes on his alcohol, Chris has a unique relationship with current, underground moonshiners. He is trusted by legal and illegal moonshiners alike to solve problems with their distillation processes and give feedback on their products.

Elise Coulter Burnette, Vice President of Marketing & Design, Coulter & Payne Farm Distillery, Owner Shawnee Bend Farms

Elise handles all design, photography, marketing, advertising, the website, and events for Coulter & Payne Farm Distillery. Beyond that, she is also a brewer and distiller for the company. She may very well be the first female distiller in

Co-author Elise Coulter Burnette, VP of Marketing and Design at Coulter & Payne Farm Distillery, climbing out of "Dolly" after a thorough cleaning.

the state of Missouri and is only one of a handful nationwide. She also consults with other distilleries on marketing issues and branding. She loves bourbon and can identify off flavors—and the probable reason—from the smell alone, before she ever takes a drink.

Elise holds bachelor of science degrees in secondary technology education specializing in industrial technology and electronic media with a minor in photography from Northern Arizona University and a master of arts in multimedia design and communications from Lindenwood University. She learned the art of distillation by working side by side with her family at the distillery and with her grandpa on the family farm. Her family has long-lived connections with the production of alcohol also starting in Jamestown Colony, including great-grandparents who were farm distillers, a grandfather who was a home brewer and winemaker, and even a law man who made money on the side bootlegging during Prohibition. Her family also owned a grain and seed company in Kirkwood, Missouri, and she has brought that back to the family by turning their farm into a non-GMO grain producer. It is one of the first small farms in Missouri to be completely non-GMO outside the Amish community.

Spirits are a passion for both Chris and Elise. It is fitting that they now own and operate a small farm distillery on their family farm. Outside of their own companies, they are also members of the Missouri Farmer's Union, the Missouri Chapter of the Sierra Club, the American Distilling Institute, the American Craft Spirits Association, and Slow Food USA, and support countless others.